D1540625

Teen Parents

THE CHANGING FACE OF MODERN FAMILIES

Teen Parents

Rae Simons

Mason Crest Publishers, Inc.

MASON CREST PUBLISHERS INC.
370 Reed Road
Broomall, Pennsylvania 19008
(866)MCP-BOOK (toll free)
www.masoncrest.com

First Printing
9 8 7 6 5 4 3 2 1

Library of Congress Cataloging-in-Publication Data

Simons, Rae, 1957–
Teen parents / Rae Simons. — 1st ed.
p. cm.
Includes index.
ISBN 978-1-4222-1491-6 — ISBN 978-1-4222-1490-9 (series)
1. Teenage parents—Juvenile literature. I. Title.
HQ759.64.S566 2010
306.8740835—dc22
2009025955

Produced by Harding House Publishing Service, Inc. www.hardinghousepages.com
Interior Design by MK Bassett-Harvey.
Cover design by Asya Blue www.asyablue.com.
Printed in The United States of America.

Although the families whose stories are told in this book are made up of real people, in some cases their names have been changed to protect their privacy.

Photo Credits

Centers for Disease Control and Prevention 20, 25; Creative Commons Attribution 2.0 Generic: lunar caustic 18, papertygre 50, Parrish, Josh 52, teresawer 11, timatymusic 34: istockphoto.com: digitalskillet 27

Contents

Introduction

The Gallup Poll has become synonymous with accurate statistics on what people really think, how they live, and what they do. Founded in 1935 by statistician Dr. George Gallup, the Gallup Organization continues to provide the world with unbiased research on who we really are.

From recent Gallup Polls, we can learn a great deal about the modern family. For example, a June 2007 Gallup Poll reported that Americans, on average, believe the ideal number of children for a family to have these days is 2.5. This includes 56 percent of Americans who think it is best to have a small family of one, two, or no children, and 34 percent who think it is ideal to have a larger family of three or more children; nine percent have no opinion. Another recent Gallup Poll found that when Americans were asked, "Do you think homosexual couples should or should not have the legal right to adopt a child," 49 percent of Americans said they should, and 48 percent said they shouldn't; 43 percent supported the legalization of gay marriage, while 57 percent did not. Yet another poll found that 34 percent of Americans feel a conflict between the demands of their professional life and their family life; 39 percent still believe that one parent should ideally stay home with the children while the other works.

Keep in mind that Gallup Polls do not tell us what is right or wrong. They don't report on what people should think—only on what they do think. And what is clear from Gallup Polls is that while the shape of families is changing in our modern world, the concept of family is still vital to our sense of who we are and how we interact with others. An indication of this is the 2008 Gallup poll that found that three out of four Americans reported that family values are important, while one in three said they are "extremely" important.

And how do Americans define "family values"? According to the same poll, here's what Americans say is their definition of a family: a strong unit where faith and morals, education and integrity play important roles within the structure of a committed relationship.

The books in the series demonstrate that strong family units come in all shapes and sizes. Those differences, however, do not change the faith, integrity, and commitment of the families who tell their stories within these books.

1 Teen Parents: The Reality

In the United States, nearly a million teenage girls become pregnant every year. These young women—and the young men who are their sexual partners—are less apt to finish high school or go on to college. Every day, they will need to make tough decisions about their priorities: should they spend their money on a CD—or diapers? Should they go out with their friends—or stay home and put the baby to bed?

Life isn't easy for teen parents. They and their children are more likely to have an income that's below the ***poverty level***. Their children are more apt be born prematurely and to have a low ***birth weight***, and they are two times more likely to suffer abuse and neglect compared to the children of older mothers.

When a teenager gets pregnant, the consequences are serious—not only for the young adults involved, but also for their children and for society as a whole.

- The sons of teen mothers are two times more likely to end up in prison than the sons of mothers who are 20 or older.
- The daughters of young teen mothers are three times more likely to become teen mothers themselves when compared to mothers who had a child when they were over 20.
- Children of teen mothers do worse in school than those born to older parents. They are 50 percent more likely to repeat a grade, are less likely to complete high school than the children of older mothers, and they get lower grades and do more poorly on tests.
- Children of older mothers are more prepared to enter the school system and score higher on measures of school readiness compared to the children of teen mothers. The children of teen mothers score lower on tests that measured thinking ability, knowledge, and language development compared to the children of older mothers. They are also less

Terms to Understand

Welfare: financial or other aid provided by the government for those in need.
aspirations: goals, objectives, dreams for the future.
abstinence: the practice of not having sexual intercourse.
scourge: a cause of trouble, pain, or disaster.
norm: a standard, general level or average.
impaired: diminished, damaged, or weakened.
permissive: characteristically accepting or tolerant of something.
inconsistent: lacking in agreement between different parts or elements.

likely to read simple books by themselves and to demonstrate early writing ability compared to the children of mothers who were older than 20.

- Children of mothers age 17 and younger are more likely to be *impulsive* or *overactive*, and to suffer from anxiety, loneliness, low *self-esteem*, or sadness.
- Almost one-half of all teen mothers and over three-quarters of unmarried teen mothers began receiving *Welfare* within five years of the birth of their first child.
- Some 52 percent of all mothers on Welfare had their first child as a teenager.
- Teen mothers are less likely to complete the education necessary to qualify for a well-paying job—only 40 percent of mothers who have children before age 18 ever graduate from high school compared with about three-quarters of similar young women who delay childbearing until age 20 or older. Furthermore, fewer than two percent of mothers who have children before age 18 complete college by the age of 30 compared to 9 percent of young women who wait until age 20 or older to have children. These difference in education also tends to affect income level: over the past 20 years the average income for college graduates has increased 19 percent while the average income for high school dropouts has decreased 28 percent.
- Nearly 80 percent of fathers of children born to teen mothers do not marry the mothers. These fathers pay less than $800 annually in child sup-

port, often because they are quite poor themselves. Since child support can be an important source of income for poor children—accounting for 23 percent of the family income among those families who do receive child support—children born to young fathers are even more likely to be poor.

Sometimes you'll hear adults talking about teen pregnancy as though it's a new and disturbing *trend*. But the reality is: teen pregnancy has always been around. It reached its highest level ever in 1991, when for every 1,000 girls between 15 and 19, there were 117 pregnancies. Teen pregnancy rates have been going down since 1992,

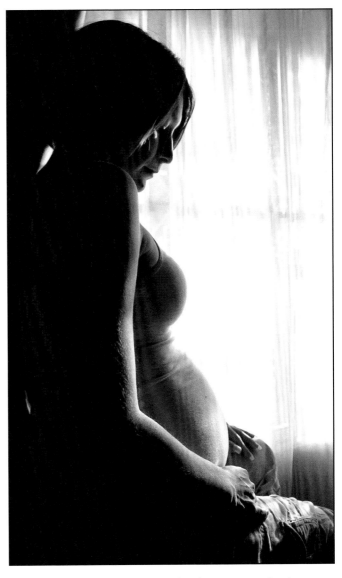

When a teenager learns she is pregnant, she has some difficult choices. Should she get an abortion, carry the baby and give it up for adoption, or raise it herself?

Ninety percent of prison inmates between the ages 15 and 19 years old are products of adolescent pregnancy.

though, and today they are about one-third lower than they were at the beginning of the 1990s. That's the good news.

The bad news is that even with this decrease in teen pregnancy, the United States still has the highest teen pregnancy rate of the *developed nations*. Three out of every ten American teenage girls will get pregnant this year.

Are these teenage parents and their children doomed to suffer all the problems described in this chapter? Of course not. Courageous young parents—like the ones who shared their stories in the chapters of this book—are working hard to beat the odds.

But it is hard work. That's the point. As you read the interviews included in this book, try to imagine yourself in each teen parent's place. Would you want to take on the challenges they faced while you're still a teenager—or would you rather wait?

HEADLINES

(Susan J. Demas, *Capitol Chronicles*, June 22, 2008)

Enough. When seventeen girls (none more than 16) at a single high school get knocked up on pact, it's time for a harsh dose of reality.

It's child abuse, plain and simple. I don't care how much these children claim they'll love their children. I'm appalled that according to a national expert, girls think of "babies as something fun" and something akin to "getting a tattoo." Where are their parents and what in God's name are they teaching these girls?

. . . Many kids have no *aspirations* and don't even plan on finishing high school. Some girls think this is a great way to get a guy to marry them. Many guys think pregnancy is strictly the girl's problem. . . . We can talk about solutions. We can talk birth control, *abstinence* and parental involvement. Right now, I'm just angry. Someone needs to speak up for the kids left behind in all this.

The reason why teen pregnancy is such a *scourge* is because we can't simply tell these boys and girls, "You screwed up. Now you pay the price." Because we all do—especially their child.

What Do You Think?

Why does the author of this editorial say she is angry? Do you think she has a right to be? Why or why not?

HEADLINES

(From David Popenoe's testimony before the House of Representatives, July 16, 1998.)

Throughout the history of the world, until the modern era, teen pregnancies were the *norm*. When a young girl became sexually mature she was married off and soon accomplished that for which she is biologically designed, giving birth to the next generation. Teen pregnancies are still the norm in much of the developing world. Each child born to a young girl normally is considered a blessing.

But in the developed nations the situation is different. The networks to help the teen mothers, composed of grandmothers, large, extended families, intimate neighborhoods, and working fathers, are seldom in existence. More importantly, women are expected to become educated and, for many, have secure employment before they bear children. Education is considered to be a necessity for living in a complex, information-rich society, and young women today are involved in the work force at about the same rate as young men.

Under modern conditions, teen pregnancies are considered not a blessing but a curse. This is so because most of the children of these pregnancies will grow up fatherless and at high risk themselves for various social and behavioral problems, the education and work lives of their mothers will be seriously *impaired*, and the welfare and social costs to the nation will be great.

With its very high teen pregnancy rate the United States is seriously out of line with other developed nations. Each year in this country almost one million teenagers become pregnant, and approximately four in ten girls become pregnant at least once before reaching the age of twenty. This is twice the rate found in the next highest nation, Great Britain, and nearly ten times the rates found in Japan and the Netherlands. Although the teen pregnancy rate in the United States has dropped some in the past few years, it is still substantially higher than in the early 1970s and the drop should not deflect us from grappling with this urgent national problem. . . .

There is a straightforward reason why the unmarried teen pregnancy rate has increased so dramatically—teens are having more sex, at earlier ages, and without the use of contraceptives. In 1970, 35% of girls and 55% of boys reported having had sex by age eighteen. By 1988, the figures were 56% for girls and 73% for boys. Today, if the data were available, the amount of teen sexual activity undoubtedly would be still higher. This is despite a slight decline over the past few years, reported by

some studies, in the stated acceptance of casual sex by young people.

One reason for the increase in teen sexual activity is that the age of puberty slowly has been dropping. But the principal reason, in my opinion, is a dramatic increase in sexually *permissive* attitudes among the young. In a recent *Wall Street Journal* poll, for example, 47% of respondents ages 18-29 said that 'premarital sex is not wrong at all,' compared to only 12% of people in the 65 and over age category. Contraceptive use has increased, but the use is often *inconsistent* and in any event is not enough to offset the increase in sexual activity.

What Do You Think?

This author says that teenage pregnancy was perfectly acceptable in other times and in other parts of the world. Why are things different for teens growing up today? How does the author explain the increase of teen pregnancy during the last part of the 20th century? Do you think he is correct? Why or why not?

2 Teen Mothers

Terri-Ann Perryman's fourteenth birthday was a disaster. She started the day by throwing up—but she'd been doing that every day for the past week, so there was really nothing special about that. "I just thought I had a stomach flu," she said. "But that morning, I came out of the bathroom and my mom was giving me the evil eye. 'Me and you are going to the doctor *right now*,' she told me. I guess she already knew what the doctor was going to tell us, but I didn't, I honest-to-god didn't know. When the doctor said I was pregnant, I started laughing, I didn't believe it was true. If the doctor hadn't been there, my mom would've probably slapped me. As it was, by the time, we got home, I wasn't laughing anymore, believe me. There was no birthday cake for me that night. I went to bed and cried myself to sleep. I couldn't believe that life could

Terms to Understand

trimester: a period of three months, especially one of the three three-month periods the human pregnancy is divided into.

grace: an act of favor or goodwill.

food stamps: coupons sold or given to needy people through government programs that can be exchanged for food at many grocery stores.

GED: General Equivalency Diploma; earned by taking a series of tests, the GED is equivalent to a high school diploma.

paternity: fatherhood; the relationship of a father to his child.

discrimination: making judgments or basing treatment on categories rather than on individual merit.

exclude: to keep out.

legitimate: genuine, authentic.

confidentiality: the state of keeping information secret.

get any worse. Shows how much you know when you're fourteen!"

Terri-Ann's pregnancy wasn't an easy one. She was sick to her stomach every day, right through her third trimester. She had just gotten on her school's JV girls' basketball team, but now she had to drop off the team.

A developing baby goes through drastic changes during the 40 weeks of pregnancy. This image shows a fetus at about ten weeks.

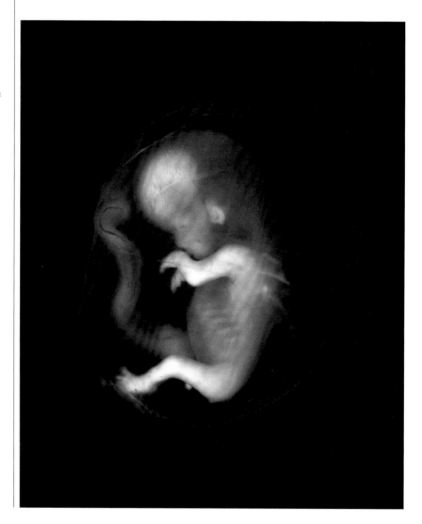

Her grades went downhill, because she missed so much school. Her boyfriend broke up with her, and her mother seemed to be constantly angry at her.

"I understand my mom better now," Terri-Ann said. "Now that my daughter is a teenager, I sure don't want her repeating my same mistakes all over again—and that's what I did to my mom. My mother had my brother when she was sixteen, me when she was eighteen—and now here I was, only fourteen, and already pregnant. She was just as angry with herself as she was at me, probably, but I didn't know that then. I thought she was an out-and-out hypocrite, condemning me for making the same mistake she had made. And I missed being my mama's baby girl, the way I had been up till then, someone she used to love up all the time. Lots of nights, I'd wake up scared, and I'd wish I could go crawl in her bed, the way I would have just a few months before, but I was pretty sure I wouldn't be welcome. So I'd lie there feeling the baby wiggle inside me, and I'd talk to the baby. I told myself that baby was going to love me more than anyone else ever had. I couldn't wait for her to be born. I couldn't wait to hold her and hug her and dress her in cute little baby clothes."

Terri-Ann's baby was born on a cold Saturday night. "I was a few weeks early, and I wasn't expecting it to be so soon. I was spending the night with some girlfriends, and I woke up in labor. I was scared stiff. I called my mom, and she came to get me right away. I always remember how glad I was to see her, I guess 'cause I knew in the end, nothing else mattered except that she was there and she was going to make sure I got to the hospital and then she made sure they took care of me. She didn't leave my side. I remember she said, 'It's bad but you get through it. Just think about next Tuesday.'

"'What's happening Tuesday?' I asked her.

"'On Tuesday you'll be bringing your baby home. Your grandma will come and see you and bring you

Trends in the Prevalence of Sexual Behaviors (Source: National Youth Risk Behavior Survey). The decline in teenage pregnancies may be due to better sexual education in school. However, about 40% of sexually-active teenagers still do not use a condom.

1991	1993	1995	1997	1999	2001	2003	2005	2007	Changes from 1991 2007[1]	Change from 2005 2007[2]
Ever had sexual intercourse										
54.1 (50.5–57.8)[3]	53.0 (50.2–55.8)	53.1 (48.4–57.7)	48.4 (45.2–51.6)	49.9 (46.1–53.7)	45.6 (43.2–48.1)	46.7 (44.0–49.4)	46.8 (43.4–50.2)	47.8 (45.1–50.6)	Decreased, 1991–2007	No change
Had sexual intercourse with four or more persons during their life										
18.7 (16.6–21.0)	18.7 (16.8–20.9)	17.8 (15.2–20.7)	16.0 (14.6–17.5)	16.2 (13.7–19.0)	14.2 (13.0–15.6)	14.4 (12.9–16.1)	14.3 (12.8–15.8)	14.9 (13.4–16.5)	Decreased, 1991–2007	No change
Currently sexually active (Had sexual intercourse with at least one person during the 3 months before the survey.)										
37.5 (34.3–40.7)	37.5 (35.4–39.7)	37.9 (34.4–41.5)	34.8 (32.6–37.2)	36.3 (32.7–40.0)	33.4 (31.3–35.5)	34.3 (32.1–36.5)	33.9 (31.4–36.6)	35.0 (32.8–37.2)	Decreased, 1991–2007	No change
Used a condom during last sexual intercourse (Among students who were currently sexually active.)										
46.2 (42.8–49.6)	52.8 (50.0–55.6)	54.4 (50.7–58.0)	56.8 (55.2–58.4)	58.0 (53.6–62.3)	57.9 (55.6–60.1)	63.0 (60.5–65.5)	62.8 (60.6–64.9)	61.5 (59.4–63.6)	Increased, 1991–2003 No change, 2003–2007	No change
Used birth control pills before last sexual intercourse (To prevent pregnancy, among students who were currently sexually active.)										
20.8 (18.5–23.2)	18.4 (16.3–20.7)	17.4 (15.2–19.8)	16.6 (14.7–18.8)	16.2 (13.6–19.0)	18.2 (16.5–20.0)	17.0 (14.7–19.4)	17.6 (15.1–20.5)	16.0 (14.2–17.9)	No change, 1991–2007	No change
Drank alcohol or used drugs before last sexual intercourse (Among students who were currently sexually active.)										
21.6 (18.7–24.8)	21.3 (19.3–23.5)	24.8 (22.1–27.8)	24.7 (22.9–26.7)	24.8 (21.8–28.0)	25.6 (23.8–27.4)	25.4 (23.2–27.8)	23.3 (21.1–25.6)	22.5 (20.7–24.5)	Increased, 1991–2001 Decreased, 2001–2007	No change
Ever taught in school about AIDS or HIV infection										
83.3 (80.1–86.0)	86.1 (83.4–88.4)	86.3 (79.0–91.3)	91.5 (90.3–92.5)	90.6 (89.1–91.9)	89.0 (87.6–90.3)	87.9 (85.8–89.7)	87.9 (85.8–89.7)	89.5 (88.1–90.7)	Increased, 1991–1997 Decreased, 1997–2007	No change

[1] Based on trend analyses using a logistic regression model controlling for sex, race/ethnicity, and grade.
[2] Based on t-test analyses, p < .05.
[3] 95% confidence interval.

presents, and your friends will be dropping by the house, and you'll be lying in bed at home, with all this over and done with. Tuesday's only a couple days away. You can handle most anything for a day or two. Just keep thinking that. As bad as the next few hours are gonna be, just remember: they won't last.'

"She was right of course. It was bad, but I don't really remember that part. I remember the first time I saw my daughter. She was just so little, this miracle, this amazing grace. And then I remember taking her home with Mom, and how tired I was and excited, all at the same time."

Over the next few months, though, Terri-Ann's excitement didn't last. She loved baby Grace, but Terri-Ann was exhausted all the time. "My grandma babysat Grace while I went to school, but Grandma was too old to help out more than that. And my mom refused to help. 'Be thankful I'm giving you and your kid a place to live,' she'd say when I'd complain that I needed her to do something for me. Grace would be up all night, screaming, and I'd want to hold a pillow over her head till she stopped. I'm serious. I truly wanted to kill that child. It terrified me. But my mom wouldn't help me. My friends would be talking about getting some new jeans or hanging out flirting with the guys—and I'd just be too tired to even care. I went to school, I came home, I took care of Grace, I tried to get some sleep, and then I did it all over again. I had never thought life could be

Teen mothers are 50 percent more likely to abuse their children. That's not because these young women are bad people. But raising a baby is hard work; it's frustrating and exhausting and it takes everything you have, both physically and emotionally. It's challenging enough for someone who's in her 20s or 30s with a good support system that includes an income and a stable partner—but for a teenage mom, motherhood can be overwhelming. Factor in the hormones that come into play after childbirth, and you have a set of circumstances that is tough for even the most mature, kindest, and most loving of teenagers.

What to Do If You Feel Like Hurting Your Child

If you're a teenage mom and you find yourself thinking about hurting your child, don't hate yourself. What you feel is completely normal, and probably every mother in the entire world has had feelings like that at one time or another. But it's important that you not give in to those feelings. Talk to someone you trust about what you're feeling (a parent, a religious leader, a teacher, a school counselor, an older friend). Check your yellow pages or the Internet for parent support agencies. Don't be ashamed to say you need help!

And when you're at the end of your rope, try one of these strategies:

- Take a deep breath... and another. Remember you are the adult and your child relies on you to protect her.

so hard. I didn't know how to be a good mother to my little girl, and I hated myself because I knew I was messing up. I hated her because she never stopped crying. I hated my mom because she wouldn't help me. All I could do was hold on and hope that some day life would get better."

Count to 10 . . . or 20 . . . before you do or say another thing.

- Put your child somewhere safe for a few minutes (his crib or playpen is fine for five or ten minutes), and then put *yourself* in a quiet time-out place. Think about why you are angry: is it your child, or is your child simply a convenient target for your anger?
- Phone a friend.
- If someone can watch your child, go outside and take a walk.
- Take a hot bath or splash cold water on your face.
- Hug a pillow.
- Turn on some music. Sing along.
- Call the child abuse prevention hotline and ask for help: 1-800-CHILDREN

When she was sixteen, Terri-Ann dropped out of school. "At first, it was just such a relief—to be able to sleep when Grace did, to not have to pretend I was a normal kid. But pretty soon I was bored with being home all day, and I was lonely. I missed seeing other people my age."

Terri-Ann's mother waited until Grace was two years old and then she told Terri-Ann it was time she found a job and started contributing to the household. "Mom

didn't believe in Welfare," Terri-Ann said. "By now I had a few friends with kids of their own, and they were all collecting Welfare, getting *food stamps*—but Mom was determined that I had to work. I was still only seventeen, and I hadn't gotten out of the habit of listening to my mother, I guess. So I got a job at the corner grocery store, where my grandma knew the owner, and I worked the cash register from eight to five-thirty every day. If I'd thought it was hard trying to be a mom and go to school at the same time, now I learned how hard it was to be a mom and work all day. I'd come home with my feet aching, and there would be Grace toddling around, looking cute. She made me laugh and I loved her to pieces. She slept through the night now, and when I remembered that I'd once wanted to stick a pillow over her head, I felt like I must have been crazy back then. I couldn't imagine hating Grace—but some days I sure did hate my mom. I just couldn't understand why she wouldn't help me once in a while. I wanted to go out and have a good time, like other girls my age, even once a month, every two months, something. I wanted a boyfriend. I wanted to dress up and look good, just once in a while. I wanted life to be easier. And it just never was. And Mom didn't seem to care. It was all, 'You made your bed, now you gotta lie in it.' She loved Gracie, but Mom wouldn't do one thing for that child. 'Ask your mama,' she'd tell her if Grace wanted something from her."

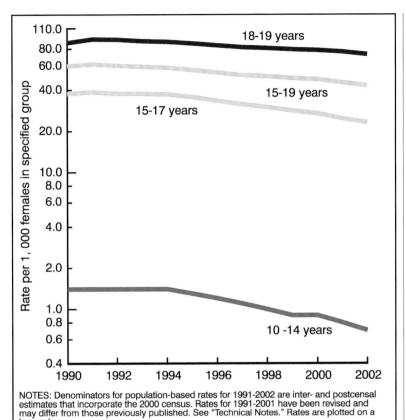

Birth Rates for Females, Age 10–19 years. Despite continuous declines over the past thirty years, the U.S. teenage pregnancy rate is still among the highest among industrialized nations.

Source: U.S. Census

The year Grace went to kindergarten, when Terri-Ann was twenty, she decided to move out of her mother's house. With Grace in school during the day, Terri-Ann's grandmother handled childcare a few evenings every week, leaving Terri-Ann with some time for herself. "I started dating Dwayne that year," she said, "and then he and I moved in together. Gracie liked him, and he was good with her. That was the first year

I remember feeling like I was really happy for a long, long time. It felt so good having someone pay attention to *me*, somehow who called me baby and brought me little presents. Dwayne was a really good guy, and I wish we could have made it work. But we didn't. I was still too young, I guess. I wanted a daddy to take care of me, to let me be a little girl again—and no twenty-one-year-old guy wants to take that on long-term, specially when there's a real baby girl in the picture. So Dwayne moved on and then it was me and Gracie again. It was tougher on Gracie than it was on me. Dwayne was like her daddy in her mind, and then he just up and left and she never saw him again. I decided I couldn't do that to her again. There'll be time enough for me to have men in my life again when she's grown. When she's eighteen, I'll only be thirty-three! It's like I've lived my whole life already, and then I'll get another chance to do it again, only better this time. At least that's what I'm hoping."

Today Grace is thirteen, and Terri-Ann is twenty-eight. "Getting my **GED** is the best thing I did for myself," Terri-Ann said. "It was tough, but it meant I could get better jobs. I like being an aide at the elementary school, and back when Gracie was younger, it meant I could keep an eye on her and be there if she needed me. I like the people I work with, and I like feeling I have a job that counts for something. I don't make a ton of money, but Grandma and Gracie and I do all right together."

Terri-Ann understands her own mother better now. "I don't know that we'll ever be close again like we were when I was young. That's sad. But I can see why she acted the way she did."

What are Terri-Ann's goals for the future? "I'd like to try to go to college when Gracie is older," Terri-Ann answered. "We'll see. Someday I'd like to get married. I'd like to have more babies, now that I've grown-up enough to handle it better. I'd like to meet a man who wants babies too, who wants to stick around and make things work. Like I said, we'll see."

What would she tell teenagers today?

An adolescent mother may feel angry that she must sacrifice much of her own childhood to care for her baby. However, she will be rewarded with happy moments as well.

Questions to Ask
If You Find Out You're Pregnant

I'm pregnant and I can't afford to go to the doctor. What do I do?

Contact your local Health Department to find out what services are available in your area. There are a lot of programs available to help you receive prenatal care. It is important to take care of yourself and the baby growing inside you.

What if my mom and dad kick me out?

A pregnant teen cannot live on her own and receive Welfare. Your parents are still legally responsible for you. They will have to pay child support for you and your child if you don't live with them.

What if I don't want to say who the dad is?

In order to get help from the Department of Health and Welfare, they will need to establish *paternity*. This is in you and your baby's best interests. Establishing paternity simply means creating a legal bond between a father and his child.

If you choose not to identify the father, you could be ineligible to receive any benefits from the Department of Health and Welfare.

What if I don't know where the dad is?

If you don't know where the dad is, you can contact the Department of Health and Welfare for help in finding him.

What do I do if the dad won't help?

It is the dad's responsibility as well as yours to support children you bring into the world. If you need assistance in getting a child support order, contact your local Health & Welfare office.

My boyfriend doesn't have a job. Will he have to quit school to pay child support?

No! It is important for everyone to complete their education. He can get a part-time job or his parents can assist in helping with child support so he can finish school. Once he turns 18 or graduates from high school, whichever comes first, he will be responsible for paying a higher amount of child support.

"Here's what I tell Gracie," Terri-Ann answered. "I say, 'I can't be with you all the time, telling you what's right and wrong. You're going to have to decide for yourself. I'm not going to be able to be there keeping you safe when some boy is cuddling you up—you're going to have to think for yourself what's best for you. You're the most amazing person in the whole world—and you better never forget it. Do what's best for you, no matter what. Be strong and think about what you really want in your life.' And then I say, 'And if you make a mistake, Gracie, I'm not gonna tell you I won't be mad—but I'll be there with you and we'll handle it together.' When a girl gets pregnant, she needs to know there are people who will help her—even if it's not her own mother, there's someone out there she can go to, places where she can get the support she needs. And really, my mom didn't do so bad—like she always said, she didn't throw me out, she kept Grace and me safe and fed and clothed. In her own way, she and I handled it together. I was lucky compared to some kids."

What is the most important thing she learned from being a teen parent? "I learned that if you just hold on long enough, things get better. When you're a teenager and your life seems like the pits, you think it's always going to be that way, that it will never end. But it does. Life keeps changing. Something new comes along.

"And here's something else I learned: that even the hardest times have their good moments—like your baby's first smile, your grandma and you laughing together, your little girl bringing you home a Mother's Day gift she made by herself, little things like that. You learn to look for those moments, to think about them instead of how tired you are or bored or lonely or just plain miserable. Teenage girls are such drama queens, and I was the same way. Being a parent made me have to grow up fast. It taught me to think about someone else besides myself."

Sharing Your Troubles

Loneliness is one of the feelings that many teen mothers share—but it helps if you can talk to other people who are going through the same thing. Check the Internet to see if there are local support groups for teen parents in your area. And if there aren't any near where you live, you can take part in online support groups. Here are a few:

The Young Mommies' Help Site
www.youngmommies.com

Bundles of Love for Young Mothers and Mothers-to-Be
bundlesoflovev2.tripod.com/

Stand Up Girl (been-there girls speak out)
standupgirl.com/web/index.php

Teen Parents Have Rights

If you're a teen parent, you have the right to:

- enroll in a GED program or a school specially suited for parenting teens—but you don't have to.
- attend school and go to class.
- access all educational opportunities that other students have.
- attend all school activities, including extracurricular activities and graduation ceremonies.
- compete on school sports teams, unless your health care provider advises you not to participate.
- miss school for *legitimate* medical appointments for you or your child.
- take a leave of absence for pregnancy, childbirth, and recovery.
- receive extra help and make up missed homework assignments due to excused absences.
- join honor societies and other academic societies if your grades qualify you.
- expect *confidentiality* when corresponding with school health care professionals.
- If you think you've been discriminated against because of pregnancy or parenthood, you also have the right to legal advice.

HEADLINES

(adapted from *Life in the Fast Lane*, the Idaho Department of Health & Welfare, www.teenageparent.org/english/teens/Leora.htm)

Leora is a teen parent; she works a part-time job, and she's also receives Public Assistance. "That's all I can do," Leora says. "Yeah, I get food stamps. I'm on Welfare and I'm not going to stay there for long. They look at you like, 'Yeah right. We know your kind. You never get out of there.'" Leora doesn't want to believe that's true about herself. It's makes her angry when people judge her.

"When we walk into the Welfare office," Leora says, "I look at people in there that are much older than I am and I think I don't want to be there. I don't. I want to be somewhere else. I don't want to have to come and [answer] to someone. I want to be able to go shopping you know, with money. Actually go cash a $600.00 paycheck. Go to the mall and buy what I want to buy and not have to think about it." Unlike other teens her age, Leora's not counting her pennies to save for a new pair of jeans; she's making sure she has enough to buy diapers and formula. She's learned the hard way that if she's not careful, she won't have enough to get through the month. "It's hard to live on a limited budget," Leora says, but she's grateful for the help she gets. She knows that some people don't

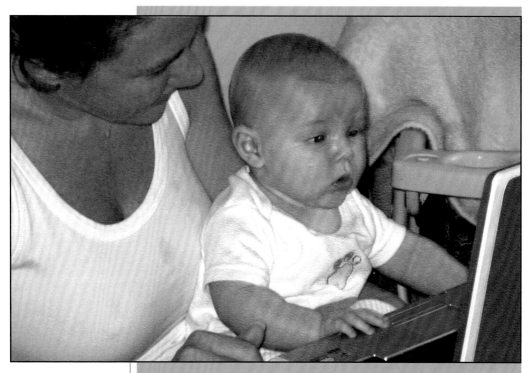

A teenage mother may find it difficult to continue her studies at the same pace as other students. A baby needs a significant amount of attention—the mother may only be able to work when her child is asleep.

like the Welfare system, but she believes it's there to help people like her who need some help. "Just use it when you need it," Leora recommends. "Don't abuse it. It's there to help us."

What Do You Think?

If you were a teen parent, would you feel embarrassed to go on Welfare? Why or why not? Ask 5 adults you know what they think about the Welfare system. Do you agree with them? Why or why not?

HEADLINES

(From Teenwire, www.teenwire.com/infocus/2006/if-20060106p405-parents.php)

As a high school student in Los Angeles, California, Cecelia (not her real name) was enrolled in a number of challenging honors courses. She took school seriously. She had to. She had plans for college, and she knew that only hard work would get her there.

So when Cecelia gave birth to a baby girl, she knew she had to find a way to keep on that path. She enrolled in a state program designed to help young parents like her finish high school. The program offered parenting classes along with childcare services. It also offered special courses designed specifically for teen mothers.

The way Cecelia saw it, there was only one problem: She didn't want "special courses." . . .

"I wanted to continue taking the college preparatory courses that I was taking before my daughter was born," wrote Cecelia in a statement provided by the American Civil Liberties Union of California, which represented her in a lawsuit filed against both the state program and Cecelia's high school district. "That wasn't possible under the way the program was being run."

Program policy forbade parenting students from taking regular high school classes. If students wanted the child-care help and other services, they were required to stick to the program's special curriculum. In other words, they were required to give up a high-quality education and take easier courses instead.

"I brought this lawsuit so that I could have the same chances and opportunities as everyone else," wrote Cecelia. "Because I have a daughter, I need those opportunities even more." Cecelia ultimately won her case, which was settled out of court, thanks to a federal law known as Title IX.

What Do You Think?

Do you admire Cecilia? Why or why not? What words do you think most describe her? (Brave? Determined? Stubborn? Self-centered? Arrogant? Mature? Intelligent?) What do you think you would have done in her place?

3 Teen Fathers

Jeremy Leahy never planned on being a father at the age of seventeen. "When I thought about my life and what lay ahead, kids weren't something I even thought about," he said.

But when Vanessa, his ex-girlfriend, told him she was pregnant, everything in Jeremy's life changed. "I didn't know what to say. I didn't know what was the right thing to do. Mostly, I just felt scared out of my mind. 'Do you want to get back together?' was the first thing I asked her, and she looked at me like I was a moron. 'No,' she told me. 'Why would I?'"

Vanessa planned to get an abortion. But when Jeremy's mother found out, she insisted that Vanessa have the baby. "My mom's pretty religious," Jeremy said. "She really believes that abortion is wrong, and she seemed more upset about the idea that Vanessa was going to have an abortion—I

Terms to Understand

fetus: the unborn young, in humans older than eight weeks after conception.

conceived: originated, began, became pregnant with.

colic: abdominal pain in infants, characterized by long periods of inconsolable crying.

family counselor: someone trained to help families dealing with difficult issues.

DNA: the molecule carrying all the genetic information of an organism.

parole: a conditional release from prison before the complete sentence has been served.

probation: a period of closely monitored freedom following or instead of time in prison.

retroactive: affecting things that have already happened or time that has already passed.

custody: guardianship, care.

access: the ability and right to have contact with.

mean, more upset than that she was pregnant in the first place. She kept saying things like, 'That little *fetus* didn't ask to be *conceived*. Someone has to look out for its rights.' It kind of freaked me out, hearing her talk about this baby's rights as though they were just as important as mine or Vanessa's. Mostly, I was just in this state of shock. I was too stunned to know what I thought or wanted. But my mom took over. She talked to Vanessa's mom, and my parents arranged to pay for Vanessa's medical expenses. In return, my parents would adopt the baby. It was all so weird. Like I said, I didn't know what to think. Things were pretty awkward between me and Vanessa. I couldn't see how it was all going to work out."

Once the baby was born—a little boy—Jeremy's mom insisted that he be the one who named him. Jeremy finally settled on the name Michael.

"At first," Jeremy recalled, "my mom was the one who took care of Michael. She got up with him in the night. She and my dad and little sister took turns walking him when he had *colic*. I just kind of hung around and watched. It was hard to believe he was really mine."

As Michael got older, though, Jeremy's mother started turning over more of his care to Jeremy. "In a way, I wanted her to," Jeremy said. "I kind of resented the way she was always in charge of Michael. I wasn't sure if she was supposed to his mother—or his grand-

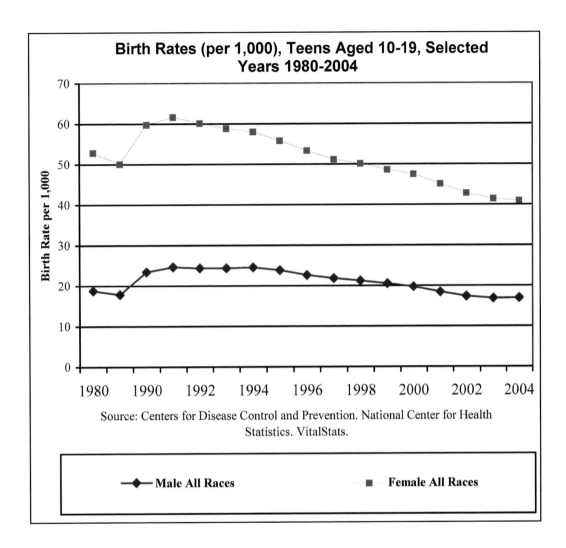

Birth Rates (per 1,000), Teens Aged 10-19, Selected Years 1980-2004

Source: Centers for Disease Control and Prevention. National Center for Health Statistics. VitalStats.

◆— Male All Races   ■ Female All Races

The numbers of teenage fathers are significantly lower than those of teenage mothers. Studies by the Population Reference Bureau and the National Center for Health Statistics found that about two-thirds of births to teenage girls in the United States are fathered by adult men age 20 or older.

Teen Fathers' Questions

What happens when I get a paternity notice?

You must respond within 10 days or you will be considered the father by default. If you have any doubts that you are the father, it is important that you get a paternity test to determine if you are or not.

How can they prove I'm a dad?

A simple test is done by comparing your *DNA* with the baby's DNA. It's quick and painless. A swab, much like a Q-Tip swab, is brushed on the inside of your mouth for cell samples to compare to the baby's.

How much child support do I have to pay?

When determining the amount of child support you have to pay, the courts examine both parents income before establishing child support orders. If you are under 18, the courts will examine not only your income, but also may include your parents' income.

Do I have to pay if I'm under 18?

It is understood that you cannot work a full-time job and concentrate on classes, but you do need to help support your child. You, and perhaps your parents, may be required to pay a smaller amount of child support until you graduate from school and can help more.

What happens if I don't pay child support?

Failure to pay child support can cause you to be in contempt of court and have your:
1. Driver's license suspended;
2. Hunting and fishing license suspended;
3. Possibly go to jail; or
4. Prevent you from getting credit.

What happens if I'm in jail? Will I still have to pay?

You have to pay while you are in jail, if you have any income. You still are responsible for your child and support. Your child support will accumulate and when you get out, it will be a condition of your *parole* or *probation* and you will need to have a plan as to how you will pay the *retroactive* support payments.

My old girlfriend won't let me see my child. What should I do?

Visitation issues need to be addressed by the parents through their local district court.

I want to get custody of my child. What should I do?

Custody issues need to be addressed by the parents through their local district court.

Teen Father's Rights

If you're a teen father, one of your most important rights is to know for sure you really are the father. The child has the right to know who his biological father is as well. Your girlfriend is going through a lot during a pregnancy, and she may be upset if you ask for a DNA test—but you don't need to feel guilty. You are not calling her sexual conduct in to question by wanting to know for sure that you are the father. You are not suggesting that she is bad or a liar. You are simply exercising your right to know for sure that you are the father and this is important because fatherhood is a lifelong commitment.

If you are in fact the father, you have the right to know your child and to participate in your child's life. You have rights of *custody* and *access*. You also have responsibilities. You have the responsibility to financially and emotionally care for your child. You have a responsibility to be present in your child's life and ensure that your child's needs are met. You have the responsibility to ensure that your child is safe and well cared for and is free from harm. You have the responsibility to make decisions that are in the best interest of your child.

mother. I wasn't sure what my role was supposed to be. Was my dad Michael's father or his grandfather? Who was I? Uncle Jeremy or Daddy? Like I said, it was just all so weird. I was trying to think about what college to go to, about getting a job so I could pay for a car—and then trying to think where Michael fit in all that."

Eventually, Jeremy and his family went to a *family counselor* who helped them sort out what was best for Michael and for everyone else in the family. "We decided I needed to be Daddy. That meant my mom and dad would help me out, but that I was the one who was really responsible for Mikey. The counselor encouraged me to take Mikey into account with every decision I made—so I ended up going to a local college and living at home, where my mom could keep on helping out with childcare. I bought a car that was safe and had plenty of room for a baby's car seat. I didn't go out at night much anymore, because it was my job now to get Mikey ready for bed. My parents and I worked out a budget, where they would help out with so much of Mikey's expenses, and I would have to take care of the rest."

What did he learn from all this? "I learned to be a whole lot more responsible. Sometimes it seemed like it wasn't fair—I didn't mean for Vanessa to get pregnant, but Vanessa moved away and went on with her life, leaving me stuck with this responsibility that was never going to go away. But most of the time, I kind of felt sorry for Vanessa. She was missing all the funny goofy things

Why Are Fathers Important?

- Children who live apart from their fathers are five times more likely to be poor than children with both parents at home.
- Boys and girls without involved fathers are twice as likely to drop out of school, twice as likely to abuse alcohol or drugs, twice as likely to end up in jail, and two to three times more likely to need help for emotional or behavioral problems.
- Teen girls who don't have a father in their life are two times more likely to begin sexual activity early and are seven times more likely to get pregnant compared to girls with fathers who take an active role in their lives.

Michael did as he got older. She was missing out on the way he felt in my arms, the way he smiled when I came home, his first words, all that stuff."

Does he regret what happened between him and Vanessa? "How could I? She and I hadn't been together, Michael wouldn't have existed. But kids need to think about what it means to have sex a lot more carefully than I did. There's always a chance of pregnancy. Even if you decide to have an abortion, there's no way you can turn back time. That pregnancy will be a part of you, one way or another, the rest of your life. So you better make sure you're ready to handle that before you start having sex. And I guess what I regret most is that Michael's life is kind of mixed up. He's going to grow up different than other kids—and I really want the best for him. So I kind of feel guilty that I messed up his life before it even started. Now we just have to do the best we can with what we have. I want him to know he can always count on me from now on. That's what's most important to me."

What Do You Think?

Compare the way Jeremy's mother reacted to the way Terri-Ann's mother did. What do you think explains the difference between the two mothers' reactions? Which mother's approach do you think was better for their children and grandchildren? Why?

HEADLINES

(adapted from *Life in the Fast Lane*, the Idaho Department of Health & Welfare, www.teenageparent.org/english/teens/Roque.htm)

Eighteen-year-old Roque takes being a father very seriously. He works hard and sends as much money as he can to his child's mother. Meanwhile, he hardly knows his daughter.

"It is hard to see my daughter since I'm separated from her," Roque explains. Because he knew his ex-girlfriend was depending on him for child support, he moved out of state in order to take a construction job with good pay. "It's hard for me to get to know her better. She's going to grow up not knowing who I am. That's a big thing that I look at. Man, I don't want her to grow up not knowing who I am because she's not going to like me because I'm her dad. 'Who is this guy coming every here and there.' It's sad because I don't want her not knowing me when she gets older. She just sees me every chance that I get to see her. She won't call me Dad; she'll be calling me by my name. That kind of thing hurts me because she doesn't know who I am."

Roque warns other teen fathers: "It's going to be hard for you because you're going to be frustrated. It's ridiculous having a kid at a young age. . . . You think everything is going to be okay, yeah, everything is going to be fine. . . [but] you don't know what to do and now everything breaks apart; your plans that you had by thinking that you were ready to have a kid, they're broken. . . . That's what you go through as you grow up. You find out what's there and what's not there."

For Roque, the future is an uncertain place. He had planned on staying together with his girlfriend, on being a family. But that hadn't worked out. "Nothing is for sure," he says with a sigh.

What Do You Think?

All the teen parents interviewed in this book eventually broke up with the mother or father of their child. Do you think that is what usually happens? Why or why not?

4 Teen Parents: The Child's Perspective

When Autumn Barron entered college, her mother did too. "I was seventeen," Autumn said. "My mom was thirty-four. I was the same age she was when she had me—and because of me, she put off going to college until I was ready to go too."

What was it like for Autumn growing up with a mom who was so young? "Sometimes it was great," Autumn said. "It was like my mom and I were this team, just the two of us against the world. We were a lot closer to each other than most of my friends were to their mothers. Sometimes I liked that, sometimes I hated it. I mean, sometimes you don't like knowing you're your mother's best friend. You wish she didn't lean on you quite so hard. You wish she could just go out with your dad, like other people's parents, and leave you a little space."

Terms to Understand

socioeconomic status: a person's position in the social structure, dependent on many variables, such as income, occupation, education, and place of residence.

biological impact: the effect of something on living organisms.

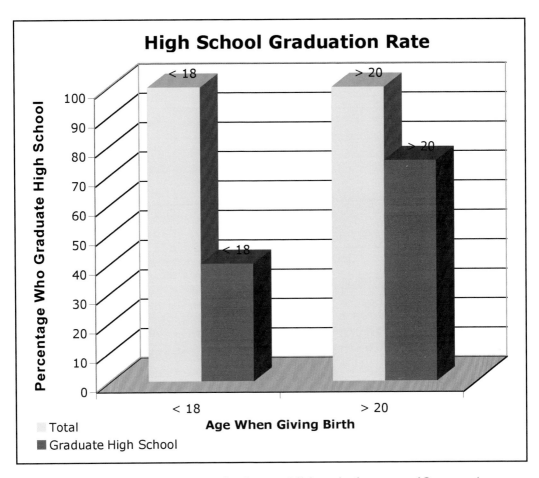

High School Graduation Rate

Only 40 percent of teenagers who have children before age 18 go on to graduate from high school, compared to 75 percent of teens from similar social and economic backgrounds who do not give birth until ages 20 or 21.

Autumn spent a lot of time with her grandparents while she was growing up. "My mom tried to work nights while I was young, so she could be there during the day with me. So I'd sleep at one of my grandparents' houses a lot of times. I didn't like that much. I remember I used to cry and ask her why she couldn't stay home at night. And then she'd be tired and grouchy a lot during the day. Now, I wonder when she ever slept, but when you're four you don't think about things like that."

Autumn also saw her dad regularly. "He took me places about once a month, like the zoo or a

The parents of a teenage parent will often play a large role in the life of their grandchild, caring for her while their child attends classes or works.

movie or something. I went through a phase when I was a teenager when I was mad at my mom all the time and I'd say I wanted to go live with my dad instead. But deep in my heart, I knew he really didn't want me full time. He loves me, and he's a good guy, and I'm glad he stuck around as much as he did—but he has his own life, and having a teenager kid wouldn't have fit in with that too well. That used to hurt a lot. I'm really grateful to my grandpa, my mom's dad, because I was always his little girl, he always had time for me, he always made me feel special. I was lucky to have him."

What was the hardest thing Autumn faced while she was growing up? "Maybe it sounds really selfish, but the hardest thing for me was when my mom ended up getting engaged when I was fifteen. I was so jealous. All those years, it had just been me and her, and now she'd brought this stupid guy into our life. I despised him, I thought he was just this complete and utter jerk. I'd be as rude to him as I dared, hoping I could drive him away. They're getting married this summer, and he and I finally get along. But I won't ever think of him as my father. If she needs him to be happy, well then, of course I want my mom to be happy. I guess I thought she should have found someone better. But like I said, I want her to be happy. She deserves to be. I know how hard she worked. I'm not saying she was perfect, but I know she really did do the best she could."

What would Autumn do if she found out she was pregnant? "I'm not going to! I'm glad my mom chose to have me—but that's something I'm never going to do. She and I spent too many years being poor, living in crummy apartments, driving cars that were always breaking down. I want a good job, a nice house, nice clothes, a nice car. Well yeah, I want a boyfriend too—

In a reversal of roles, a daughter proudly attends her mother's college graduation. As she gets older, a child of a teenage mother will better appreciate the sacrifices her mother made.

but I'm not going to risk getting pregnant until I'm sure I've got all the other pieces in place. Maybe that makes me sound selfish, but that's what I feel like. I don't need any boy as much as I need to know I can take care of myself. I guess that's what my mom taught me."

HEADLINES

(From the *Journal of Epidemiology and Community Health*, 17 February 2009)

Scientists have found that early parenthood can increase the chance of suffering from heart disease later in life in both men and women. Lifelong lower *socioeconomic status*, lower educational levels, and subsequent poorer lifetime health behaviors may be the pathway by which early parenthood is related to poorer health. . . . Men as well as women who became parents as teenagers had higher levels of obesity, higher blood pressure and worse cholesterol levels at the age of 53 years compared with those who became parents for the first time at an older age.

This can be largely explained by poorer health behaviors and lower socioeconomic status of young mothers and fathers so the findings show that lifestyle factors, rather than the *biological impact* of pregnancy, explain

the relationship between age at motherhood and risk factors.

Lead researcher Dr. Rebecca Hardy from the MRC Unit for Lifelong Health and Ageing said:

"We expected to see both the biological effects of early pregnancy and the influence of poorer health behaviors in young mothers having an effect on later health but to see that men who became teenage parents also had poorer heart health risk factors was an important finding. It suggests that we need to consider the family as a whole and encourage lifestyle changes, such as a healthier diet and increased exercise to improve the risk of coronary heart disease."

What Do You Think?

How does this article explain the connection between heart disease and being a teen parent? Does this make sense to you? Why or why not? What can teen parents do to counteract the risks of heart disease?

HOW MUCH DOES IT COST TO HAVE A BABY?

Add up the following costs to find out how much a baby will cost just in the first year of life.

Before Your Baby Arrives

1. You will need to buy at least 8 months' worth of prenatal vitamins! ($15.00 for 1 month's supply)
2. You will need to buy an infant car seat to take the baby home from the hospital. (You can't leave without one!) ($45.00)
3. You will need a crib. (at least $100.00 each)
4. You will need a crib mattress. (at least $45.00 each)
5. You will need at least 2 crib sheets. ($10.00 each)
6. You will need at least 2 crib blankets. ($10.00 each)
7. You will need at least 2 crib mattress pads. ($7.76 each)
8. You will need about 5 receiving blankets. ($2.98 each)
9. You will need a changing table. (at least $89.00 each)
10. You will need changing table pad(s). ($8.00 each)

Optional Nursery Items

1. A crib mobile. (at least $14.95 each)
2. A crib activity center. (at least $12.57 each)
3. A cradle or bassinette. (at least $80.00 each)

Health /Safety Items
(Remember, you are buying for a year!)

1. You will need hairbrush(es) and comb(s) for the baby. ($6.87 each)
2. You will need digital thermometer(s). ($10.27 each)
3. You will need humidifier(s)/vaporizer(s) ($35.42 each) for when the baby gets sick and you probably ought to pick up nasal aspirator(s) ($2.01 each) and medicine dropper(s) ($1.97 each).
4. You will need baby monitor(s), so you can hear when the baby is crying. ($25.00 each)
5. Do you have stairs in your house? You will need stairway gate(s) to protect the baby from falling down the stairs. ($9.96 each)
6. You will need drawer latches ($ .25 each) and outlet plug covers ($ .10 each) so the baby doesn't get into things he/she shouldn't.
7. You will need a baby bathtub. ($14.39 each)
8. You will need baby washcloths. ($ .79 each) (Don't forget to get enough for when you haven't had time to do the laundry!)
9. You will need to buy enough of each item for the year (so 3 to 5 of each):
   - baby soap ($2.77/bottle)
   - baby lotion ($2.81/bottle),
   - baby powder ($2.00 each)
   - baby oil ($2.80/bottle),
   - diaper rash ointment ($3.50/tube)

10. You will need to buy laundry detergent for baby clothes. ($4.89/box) (You'll probably go through about 2 a month!)

Diapering Needs

1. If you decide to use disposable diapers (most mothers do), your baby will go through about 6 diapers a day during the first 6 months of his or her life, a little fewer as the baby gets older. That's about 180 diapers a month—which is going to cost you about $50–$100, depending on whether you use brand name diapers or buy in bulk.
2. Even if you are using disposables, cloth diapers come in handy as burp/spit cloths. Many mothers like to keep a dozen on hand. ($12.00/dozen)
3. You will need about 2 boxes of baby wipes per month. ($2.97 each) You will need to buy diaper bag(s). ($15.00 each)

Feeding Your Baby

1. If you plan on breast-feeding your baby:
   - You will need to buy breast pump(s) if you plan on nursing while you are in school or working. ($24.98 each)
   - You will need to buy nursing pads.
     ($ .58 each, about 3–4 a day)
   - You will need to buy at least 3 nursing bras. ($at least 14.00 each)

2. If you plan on using formula:
   - You will need to buy cans of formula. ($3.65 each, 7–8 a week and about 32 a month)
   - You will need to buy bottles. ($1.65 each)
   - You will need to buy a bottle brushes to clean the bottles. ($2.00 each)
   - You will need to buy nipples for the bottles.

As Your Baby Gets Older

1. Your baby will need a toddler car seat. ($55.00)
2. At about 6 months, most babies begin to eat solid food. You will need to buy about 30 jars of baby food each week. ($ .47 each)
3. You will need a high chair. (at least $47.00 each)
4. You will need to buy childproof plates and bowls. ($3.96 each)
5. You will need to buy infant spoons. ($ .94 each)
6. You will need to buy bibs. ($2.75 each)
7. You will need to buy no-spill cups. ($1.73 each)

Clothing

Remember, every few weeks or months, your baby will grow into a new size. So you are going to need the following items for each size:

1. At least 4 or 5 sleepers. ($4.95 each)
2. At 2 or 3 hats. ($2.78 each)

3. At least 3 or 4 pairs of booties and/or socks. ($2.39 each)

4. At least 4 or 5 nightgowns. ($6.00 each)

5. At least 4 or 5 outfits. ($12.00 each)

6. A snowsuit. ($24.00 each)

7. At least 4 or 5 warm sweaters. ($18.00 each)

8. At least 4 or 5 shirts. ($6.45 each)

9. At least 4 or 5 pairs of pants.($9.18 each)

Additional Items to Make Your Life Easier—and Your Baby's Life More Fun

1. A frontpack for your baby. ($40.00 each)

2. A stroller. (at least $48.00 each)

3. A play yard. (at least $60.00)

4. A baby swing. ($80.00 each)

5. A doorway jumpers. (at least $20.00 each)

6. Small toys. (about $8.00 each)

7. Books. (at least $3.00 each)

8. Yard toys. (at least $48.00 each)

So when you add it all up, what does it come to? How much money will you need each week to be able to pay for your child?

Find Out More
BOOKS

Davis, Deborah, ed. *You Look Too Young to Be a Mom: Teen Mothers on Love, Learning, and Success.* New York: Perigee, 2004.

Endersbe, Julie K. *Teen Mothers: Raising a Baby.* Mankato, Minn.: Capstone Press, 2000.

Gottfried, Ted. *Teen Fathers Today.* Brookfield, Conn.: Twenty-First Century Books, 2001.

Goyer, Tricia. *Life Interrupted: The Scoop on Being a Young Mom.* Grand Rapids, Mich.: Zondervan, 2004.

Haskins-Bookser, Laura. *Dreams to Reality: Help for Young Moms: Education, Career, and Life Choices.* Buena Park, Calif.: Morning Glory Press, 2006.

Lindsay, Jeanne Warren. *Teen Dads: Rights, Responsibilities, and Joys.* Topeka, Kan.: Topeka Bindery, 1999.

Lindsay, Jeanne Warren. *Your Baby's First Year: A Guide for Teenage Parents.* 3rd ed. Buena Park, Calif.: Morning Glory Press, 2004.

Lipper, Joanna. *Growing Up Fast.* New York: Picador, 2003.

Paschal, Angelia. *Voices of African-American Teen Fathers: I'm Doing What I Got to Do*. Binghamton, N.Y.: Haworth Press, 2006.

Pollock, Sudie. *Will the Dollars Stretch?: Teen Parents Living on Their Own*. Buena Park, Calif.: Morning Glory Press, 2001.

ON THE INTERNET

Fact Sheets for Teen Parents
www.teenparents.org

Life in the Fast Lane: Idaho Department of Health and Welfare Web page on Teen Parenting
www.teenageparent.org

MELL: Mentor, Encourage, Lift, and Love: Providing Life Skills and Educational Workshops to Teen Parents
www.mentorencourageliftandlove.org

Teen Wire: Sexuality and Relationship Issues for Teens
www.teenwire.com

The Young Mommies Help Site
www.youngmommies.com

Bibliography

Card, J.J. *Guidebook: Evaluating Teen Pregnancy Prevention Programs*. Los Altos, Calif.: Sociometrics, 2001.

Cherry, A.L., M.E. Dillon, & D. Rugh (eds). *Teenage Pregnancy: A Global View*. Westport, Conn.: Greenwood Press, 2001

Demas, Susan J.. "Editorial." *Capitol Chronicles*. June 22, 2008.

Egendorf, L.K. (Ed.) *Teens at Risk: Opposing Viewpoints*. San Diego, Calif.: Greenhaven, 2000.

Idaho Department of Health & Welfare. *Life in the Fast Lane*. www.teenageparent.org/english/teens/Roque.htm.

"Rights for Teen Parents." Teenwire, www.teenwire.com/infocus/2006/if-20060106p405-parents.php

"Teen Pregnancy." *Journal of Epidemiology and Community Health*. February 17, 2009.

Wong, J. & D. Checkland, *Teen Pregnancy and Parenting: Social and Ethical Issues*. Toronto: University of Toronto Press, 2000.

Index

About the Author and the Consultant

AUTHOR

Rae Simons came from a family of five children, and she now has three children of her own. Her role in her "nuclear" family as well as in her extended family continues to shape her life in many ways. As a middle school teacher, she worked closely with a wide range of family configurations. She has written many educational books for young adults.

CONSULTANT

Gallup has studied human nature and behavior for more than seventy years. Gallup's reputation for delivering relevant, timely, and visionary research on what people around the world think and feel is the cornerstone of the organization. Gallup employs many of the world's leading scientists in management, economics, psychology, and sociology, and its consultants assist leaders in identifying and monitoring behavioral economic indicators worldwide. Gallup consultants help organizations boost organic growth by increasing customer engagement and maximizing employee productivity through measurement tools, coursework, and strategic advisory services. Gallup's 2,000 professionals deliver services at client organizations, through the Web, at Gallup University's campuses, and in forty offices around the world.